Birdie in the Wildwood

Birdie in the Wildwood

Michon Smith Balcome

CONTENTS

DEDICATION vii
PREFACE ix

1 Chapter 1 1
2 Chapter 2 5
3 Chapter 3 11
4 Chapter 4 15
5 Chapter 5 21

EPILOGUE 29
OLIVE BIRDIE AUSTIN SMITH 31
CLARENCE & OLIVE BIRDIE SMITH 33
POEMS BY: OLIVE BIRDIE AUSTIN SMITH 35

DEDICATION

This book is dedicated to the loving memory of my Grammy, who I admired most. Thank you for being my greatest inspiration. This book would not have been possible without you. May you be proud.

PREFACE

This narrative was written by Olive Birdie Austin Smith, my great-great grandmother. She talks about her childhood and the stories her mother told her about their family lineage.

It was eventually presented to my Grandmother, Roberta Smith Andrist. The writings of Grandma Birdie were one of my Grandma's greatest treasures that she had always hoped to share one day. She was unable to decipher the handwriting, so she tucked it away in her cedar chest for safekeeping. Over the years, she would pull it out of the cedar chest and ask if I could transcribe it. Unfortunately, I would not be able to decipher the handwriting either, and it would be returned to the cedar chest to patiently wait to one day be transcribed and shared.

In 1997, Olive Bird's daughter Margie Bartel and my grammy made the decision to compile Grandma Birdie's writings into a memory book with the help of Margie's daughter, Sharon. Grandma Birdie's story was a family legacy; therefore, they wanted to make sure everyone in the family knew about it.

My mother, Bernita Andrist Reding, informed me a few years after Grandma Roberta's death that she possessed a copy of the memory book containing Grandma Birdie's narrative. I informed her that when I was a young child, I had attempted multiple times to decipher her memoir but had failed. Knowing how special it was to my Grandma, she offered to let me try again. I was shocked to find that I could successfully transcribe Grandma Olive Birdie's narrative after several weeks of effort!

I have not altered the grammar, spelling, or wording in this memoir because it is not mine to change, and I feel that it showcases the dialect of the area that Birdie grew up in as well as the era. The story you are about to read is not only a piece of family history; it is a testament to the times and tells of the everyday hardships that American Settlers went through to try to survive and make a better life for their families.

1

Chapter 1

January 3rd 1958

Years ago I promised my husband Clair, that some day I would write what I have ben told by my good Mother, of my ancestory on her side of the ancestral tree. Also I mean to tell here the incidents of my childhood and life that I think would be of interest to my descendants. Of my mothers Grandmother I only know her parents were here in the East, before the revolution.

That my Great Great Grandfather was prominent enough to have had a price on his head by the English, that he had Traitor neighbors who plotted to capture him, and after the war was over, bragged about how he and an indian lay in ambush for him late one afternoon when they thought he would be coming for his cows. Cattle in those days had free range, and wore a bell so the owner could hear and get them at night. The Tory and the Indian hid themselves in the top brush of a big down tree and waited for my ancestor to come for his cows but they were disappointed, because his daughter came for the cows, even walked aways up the trunk of the down tree where they were hid, to look and listen for the cows. The Tory told later that he would have taken the girl prisoner, hoping by so doing to get her father when he would come to look for her, but the Indian said "not so", "no want girl" "just man, girl go home again." So the Indian had a white heart under a red skin, and the white man had a black heart in disguise of a white man.

About the only easy transportation in those days was by horseback, and the settlers had some noble and high bred riding horses. This same girl had ben away from home one day, and dark fell before she was near home. Following the trail as those roads were known, securely on top of her beautiful mount, she heard a cry in the distance like the voice of a woman, calling. She paid little attention thinking someone was calling their cows. Later the cry came again, and the horse shivered slightly, but trotted on in the usual pace, but when the call came once more much nearer, the horse gave a start and shook with fear. My lady knew then that a Panther, or mountain lion, was on her trail, and she let her horse out and lay flat on his neck, thinking, "When I have to stop to let down the gate into the field, the cat will get me", but she did not know her mount or the strength of his mighty frame, because she never knew when she reached the gate, her horse cleared it in his flight, and took her to her fathers door. This woman lived in her old age with her daughter (my Grandmother Johnston) in New York State, as it was then called, and told this story to my mother and her brothers and sisters. Her married name at that time was Hallstead. I have often heard my mother refer to "Grandma Hallstead". But I do not know the name of her father, and have a faint remembrance of that being the name of her second husband. My Grandmother Johnstons given name was Phoebe but I do not know, or never heard her last or maiden name. She was born in Onondaga Co. New York in 1816. At the age of 15 she gave her heart to God, and joined the Free Will Baptist Church, in which faith she died in 1878 at Calumet Harbor, Fond du Lac Co.Wisconsin.

My Grandfather - Thomas Johnston was born 1821 on July 4th, probably in New York, as his father owned land near the city of New York, and had extensive apple orchards, and sold apples by the barrel, also made apple cider by the barrel too, probably how my Grandfather learned how to drink and drink he surely did. My Great Grandfather bought him a farm, had it put in Grandmothers name so Tom, as he was called couldn't drink it up. But Grandfather got the moving bug, as so many early settlers did and he tormented Grandma to sell until he wore her out, and she consented and they sold their farm, loaded the family in a covered wagon and immigrated to near Fond du Lac Wisconsin. At one time they lived on the Lake Shore. Grandfather was a basket maker by trade, and I still possess one of the baskets he made while living with my Father and Mother in Pine Co. at about the age of 89 or 90. Later my parents came to live at Mantorville for a couple of years, and Grandpa died there, in a big house known at that time as the Sanford house.

When my parents lived there, there was stored in the upstairs some massive Black Walnut, antique Bedsteads. Now 50 years later they would be worth quite a lot of money, as they were then in excellent condition. Grandpa was taken to Pine City and buried in the family lot, where my brother Tom was also buried years before. But that remains to be told.

My Mother was a timid woman in thunder storms but if crowded by circumstances was as brave as most women would be. She was born in New York, near where the great City stands now, in 1846, and came to Wisconsin with her family while a small girl.

my mother was a timid woman in thunder
storms but if crowded by circumstances was as
brave as most women would be.
She was born in New York, near where the great
City stands now, in 1846, and came to wisconsin
with her family while a small girl.

Her Mother was Scotch and Irish, and her Father was Holland Dutch (or American Dutch) as I suppose he was born in New York also, and have no reason to think otherwise. My Grandparents had a large family, I think my Mother said Grandma gave birth to sixteen children, some died at birth and some at an early age. The family were very poor and the childrens education was sketchy because they so many times did not have proper clothes, and as the family had to furnish their own school books at that time, and education was not compulsory. They were not kept in school as children as these later days. Grandmother was a good house keeper, and her girls were well trained to keep house in poverty and hardship, and hard work.

When Grandfather would come home drunk, Grandma would hide in the willows along the Lake shore and the children's hide outs were numerous, as the children themselves. My Mother grew up a fine healthy girl with hazel eyes and thick long brown hair, as long as a mans arm and the coil as thick as his wrist. When her hair was down she could sit on it. It was fine, silky and straight as an Indians. She used to tell us children funny tales about her girlhood, and one that has remained in my memory, the funniest of all, was when she was a big girl, and went to help an old German neighbor woman, and she sent Mother into the pantry to skim the milk and it was set on a long shelf to rise, in a row of chamber pots. The son of the lady of the house was sweet to Mother, but the milk deal cooked his goose then and there. Another story she told us, was about a girl she knew who worked for a Dr. and one day while cleaning house she opened the closet door to the Dr's private room, and discovered the body of a person she knew had ben buried the day before. That night she went home, and became deathly sick, but before she died of poison she told of what she saw in the Dr's room. Grave robbing by Dr's was more common than it is of this date in history. If she told what was done with the Dr. I can't remember.

Mother was married soon after the close of the Civil War. My Father and her brother were "Buddies".

2

Chapter 2

Of my Fathers family I know very little as his Mother died when he was five years old and his Father married again, and had children by his second wife, but when Grandpa Austin died when father was about 9, he went out on his own, as his step Mother was unkind to him and he never got enough to eat, or clothes to wear for comfort. And as he was rather crippled having ben dropped and getting a bad hip injury when he was a baby. People were kind to him and took him in, and he learned the carpenters trade, and was clever at wood work, it being his greatest talent.

He enlisted in the Army when the Civil War broke out, and was mustered out at the close, having languished in a Southern concentration camp eleven months, having escaped once from Andersonville, and was out 40 days and nights, and was trying to get back to the Union Lines when he was recaptured, and this time went to the vile prison at Belle Isle. He never recovered from the starvation he experienced there. He was always hungry, but I never saw him go to Mothers cupboard and lunch between meals, and he never kept meals waiting for him as so many men sometimes do. But if Mother put out food for him, he could always eat. Mother baked the best corn bread I ever ate, and I never have ben able to match her pumpkin pies. Mother gave birth to nine children, three of whom died at birth. The first baby was a boy and died at birth. Two sons and a daughter followed and then a girl baby that died at birth. Then two more sons and a daughter (the writer) then a darling boy, about 1886. I can recall seeing him in his little casket, when my father held me up to see him, and told me we couldn't keep him because he was dead. I remember that I was sorry and in my little heart wished that he had lived, so I could have cared for him. And later when I had some little aprons from cloth that looked like the dress he wore in his casket, I knew mother had made them of the dresses he would never wear, and I asked no questions about them.

My father came of a family of Boat builders. His father was Scotch and French. His Grandfather married a French woman, and my Grandfather Austin married an English woman (Great Grandpa Austin was a boat builder on the river Clyde in Scotland). So my Father was a mixture of Scotch, French, and English. My Mother being Holland Dutch, Scotch, and Irish, I am more of a mixture than he was, but I am glad I am, and I hope I have some of the good qualities of each nationality. Recently a store keeper asked me my nationality. I told him of my mixed blood, of he said, "You are a kind of league of nations" a rare compliment, I think.

My Father built the finest row boats I ever have seen. One person could stand on the gunwale of his family boats, and not capsize it. My parents lived in what was called Mankato woods, at the time of the Indian Massacre, and Mother told of the huge Gallows, where the Indians were hanged. Later my people moved to Worthington Nobles Co. Minn. There I was born in the town of Worthington. Came near being a comic Valentine, as I was born Feb. 13th on my Mothers birthday and my Father named me Olive, after his Mother, whose maiden name was Olive Green, and he gave me the middle name "Birdie" for the tiny girl who brought him food while he was in hiding while out of prison those forty days, as he was sheltered by a family of Union Sympathizers who did not dare take the Union side, being too far south. So, Birdie I was, to my family, and to Clair, my husband, and to my old friends, who still call me "Birdie". But when I had to take over the estate at Clair's death, my attorney told me I would have to use my official name of Olive, so now I get letters addressed to Mrs. C.E. Smith, Mrs. Clair Smith, Mrs. Birdie Smith, and Olive B. Smith. What more could I desire?

My folks lived in the town of Worthington, Nobles Co. at the time I was born Feb. 13th 1881. My oldest sister Modora, and I were both born with curly hair, as was all of the boys but Herman the oldest, his hair was straight like Mothers, and he had hazel eyes like Mothers, but not her disposition. Mother was a very modest, jentle woman. She told me the woman who washed and dressed me at birth, came and carried me off one day to show me to the neighbors. My hair she said was so long she curled it. The neighbor kept me away so long that mother became worried, and Jim my brother was crying because they carried off his baby sister. So Mother went out and hunted me up. She nursed all six children, and probably thought I would be hungry, and no doubt I was.

My family lived on a farm near Worthington for a few years, not very many, as I was "still in arms" so to speak when they loaded the family into a covered wagon and traveled to "some happier" place to make a home. While they were living on their farm which was on the Prairie. They burned hay bundles for fuel, wood being too scarce and expensive for poor families. Once Father was twenty miles from home in the winter, and it came up cold, and a terrible blizzard blew up. Father knew Mother could not dig hay to burn, from the snow, so he started out with his ox team to travel the 20 miles to get home before his family froze to death. It was so cold he had to walk to keep from freezing himself, and he walked in the lead of the team, or the shelter of them, and before he got home Mother was burning the furniture. The chairs came first, and the small objects. She was to start burning the bedsteads the next day, but he arrived in the night. She said when she stepped out of bed the first morning of the blizzard the snow was ankle deep on the floor. Having sifted into the cracks in the night. Later the hair came off the ox that was on the windy side of the team, he having his hide frozen on the trip.

Blizzards in winter, and grasshoppers in summer, along with hail that also destroyed all the crops, caused Father to abandon farming in

Nobles Co. So loading the covered wagon and the family one day, they started out across the trackless prairie, seeking a better place for the struggle for existence.

None of this is in my memory, as I was a babe in arms when they left Worthington. They drove all night the first night, it having ben so late in the day when they were ready with their six children. So came morning and they stopped for breakfast and to rest and feed the oxen, and Mother being the curious one of the family, walked to a small hill to look out over the Prairie, and was astonished to see below, on the lower land, the farm house and all, they had left the day before.

The oxen, being more oriented in the night than the driver, had circled back toward the house. This couldn't have amused them at the time but in later years Mother who had a great sense of humor, told it laughing, as tho it were a great joke, which of course it was.

The Oxen, being more oriented in the night than the driver, had circled back tward house, This couldn't have amused them at the time, but in later years mother who had a great sence of humor, told it laughing, as tho it were a great joke, which of course it was.

How long they traveled before finding an empty house I have no record or account of. My first memory was living on the bank of the St. Croix River in Wisconsin in a big three story house built for a hotel to accommodate people crossing the Ferry at that place, and for the River Drivers who came with the log drives in the spring. The River drivers had a house boat called a Wanigan, an Indian name. That was before the Indians had ben forced to the Reservations, and they came and went more than was comfortable for my mother being so soon after the Mankato Massacre. She had little confidence in them.

One night there was an encampment of Indians near enough the house that the folks could watch their "Pow wow," some unholy soul had given, or sold, them some "white mans fire water", which made them drunk, and so more dangerous, but they fought only among themselves, but Mother had no rest that night, she walked from window to window all night, fearing for herself and her children.

I think Father would have made it warm for an Indian who would have tried any tricks, as he had a 44 repeating Winchester rifle, which was always loaded and ready for emergency. And we small fry were well aware of danger if we meddled with the guns in our house. I guess I never touched one until I was in my teens.

I also remember Adolph (Amos) and I were not allowed to play on the bank of the river, and I was forbidden to go upstairs. There were so many bedrooms and two long stairways, and I was so tiny. I recall standing at the foot of the downstairs, and looking up, wondering what would "get me" if I ventured up there alone. Some one must have scared me with tales to keep me from climbing up stairs.

Down the river a quarter mile or so, was a huge rock, standing well out from the shore that caused log jams if the River Drivers were not there to fend them off. My two older brothers, Herman and Tom could go in the river, as they could swim. One day Tom climbed on a rock, and it started out in deep water with him, and he hurriedly jumped off. What he had stood on was the back of a huge turtle, and it didn't care for a rider. It was while living in this house that Mother decided that two heads of long curls was too much for a mother of six and occasional borders to care for. So one day while Father was away she shingled (cut short) Dora's and my long curly hair. I can't imagine what my Father said when he saw what she had done as our curls were his pride and joy, and we inherited our curly hair from him, and he never quite forgave poor Mother for our loss of curls as when it grew out she began to braid it and that took out most of the curl. But when it was free it flowed in waves to below our waists. Father spent one winter with me years after Mother passed away and he was still mourning for my curly hair. Poor Mother, there was a limit to what one small woman could do. Mother was fine boned, but carried too much weight. She wore a four and a half shoe, and at one time weighed two hundred pounds. Yes she was a small eater and never ate lunch at home.

I think I inherited my Grandmother Johnstons build, because when Grandpa Johnston lived with me a few days while Mother got his house settled in Mantorville, he used to call me his "Scotch Lassie", and once when I did a small kindness for him, he kissed my hand. Poor old timer, he must have had a lot of things to remember and regret. He was a big man, around six foot in his youth and heavy bodied in his old age. I never had a Grandmother, both having died in middle age.

3

Chapter 3

To return to my early childhood and the big house at the Ferry. The place was called Rice's Ferry, and was owned by a man named Charley Rice. From this place we moved into a house owned by this same Charley Rice. About six miles from Pine City, near the road known then as the "Saint Croix Road". About that time there was a mill on the road, not far from the house. It was a saw mill and I can remember seeing piles of saw dust, as we went past there to Pine City. When my Father bought his farm about one and one half miles south, and a little west of the mill site. They had planned to build a school there also, and to make a settlement there, but the school fell threw, the mill failed to be a paying business, and we and some other early settlers were left to do the best we could.

Living in the Rice house with us at the time I remember, was a man named Matt, an Englishman, his last name I won't mention. He is simply "the Englishman" the meanest man I have ever known. With him was his young wife Liza, and later the baby. Having six children, my parents lived in the main part of the house, and Matt and Liza in the lean to kitchen. I remember Liza wore bangs, and as I was very tiny, about three I think, I wanted bangs too, "like Liza". So one day I hid behind the house with my little blunt scissors I used to cut paper, and pulled down some loose hair over my forehead, and snipped it off. My Father was sick in bed at the time as he so often was, being disabled in the war from walking off a cliff one dark night, while on patrol. When I appeared with my "bangs" my Father was very stern with me, and told me to go out and get a whip and bring it to him so he could whip me. I never dared to disobey my father, so I went out, and broke a switch about the size and weight of an oat straw, and took it to him. Of course I couldn't feel it thro my skirts and dress, but I cried very hard, to make him think I was hurt, and I was, my pride in my bangs was spoiled. And I have detested bangs on anyone since that day. I remember I had just one treasure, a tiny china white hen, about the size of our modern salt and pepper shakers. Mother made pockets in my aprons or dresses, and I carried my precious little hen around with me in my pocket. I made little nests for it and told myself how she was setting and would have some eggs and little chickens. And then I lost it somewhere, found it and lost it the second time, and never did find it again. I don't know how or why the part that Matt and Liza lived had dirt on the roof, but it did, and the eves was very low. One day while Father and Mother was away (they did not leave us alone often) we were playing near the eves of Matts part of the house, and one of the boys, I can't say which one, tapped the roof with his hand and we heard dirt rattle down inside, and out came Matt, mad as a hornet and he told us if we ever did so again he would cut our hearts out. Gave us a scare at any rate. Mother kept a few hens so as to have eggs to use, and Matt had a garden. The two didn't work out too well, as Mothers hens found good scratching in the garden. One day while Father was having one of his sick spells, Mother went out in the morning to split some kindle to start breakfast. Matt thought it a good time to pick on mother while Dad was sick in bed, so he started out, and raised a cow, Mother of course sassed back. He picked up a club and said "I'll show you" and Mother raised her ax, and said "If you strike me, I'll split you open" He said, "I'll go and throw all your darn stuff out", and started for the door. When he arrived there he met Father with his revolver. He had crawled out of bed when he heard the rumpus, armed himself, and met the Englishman at the door. He said "Set one foot in this house and I'll shoot you" and I know he would have too. All this we children heard from upstairs, and a row of small faces ringed the stove pipe hole in the chamber floor. I can still see my fathers revolver in hand at the door, and the amazed Matt on the door step.

Not long after that my folks moved into a house about 4 miles south of that one, owned by a man named Turner Hawk. (Where we lived at the time of Diphtheria). The boys teased me before we moved, telling me that "Hawks eat Birds" and as I was a Birdie, he might eat me. Somehow I was not very scared. I do remember I cried because they couldn't find my kittie when we moved, and my mother said "Don't cry, the cat will follow the oxens tracks and come to us". And a couple of days later the cat showed up. Whether she followed us, or the older boys sought her out I don't know.

I do not know how long we lived at Hawks place, one summer at least, because my oldest brother Herman, came down with Diptheria. This was a terrible ordeal for my parents. Herman and Father had ben on foot to Rock Creek, some three or four miles from home, and on the way home they stopped at the home of John Crawford, to rest awhile before coming on home.

While there Herman became quite sick and they stayed the night. When they managed to get a Dr. (probably from Rush City.) He told them it was Diphtheria. Herman was too sick to be moved, so Dad and Mother had to one of them be there all the time and some of the time both of them were there.

While there Herman became quite sick and
they stayed the night. When they managed
to get a Dr. (probably from Rush City.) He
told them it was Diptheria, Herman was too
sick to be moved, so Dad and mother had to
One of them be there all the time and some
of the time both of them were there,

Someone had to be with we younger children, so Crawfords sent their older girl, about sixteen I think, and she and Turner Hawk looked after us until the crisis was past, and Mother could be home with us.

Of course the Crawford children took the disease, and one little girl died, and as could be expected Father paid the Dr. bill for them, and the burial expenses, along with his own Dr. bill. It did not break up the friendship of the two families, as one might have expected. We were always the very best of friends as long as we were near enough to visit back and forth.

I lost track of Grace, the youngest daughter in 1948. After the floods in Oregon, I never heard from her again. Tho I sent a letter to her old address, it was returned stamped "unknown". I assume she is either dead or has forgotten me.

I think some of we younger children at home were sick at the time Herman was, as I remember we were kept in bed for a few days. We each had a tiny bag of assofetia about our neck, to ward off the Diphtheria germs. And a peeled onion hung from the ceiling, and I remember it turned black.

Anyway we were not dangerously sick like Herman was. He had an abscess in his throat, and the Dr. told my parents, "When it breaks if it goes down and he swallows it, he will die, but if it comes up he will live," and it did come up, and he lived to be seventy two years old and dropped dead of heart disease in New York City. Last year 1957, his youngest daughter Helen also died of Heart Disease.

The Diphtheria affair made a big hole in Fathers back pension, but he had enough left to make a down payment on some land, and to begin a house, which we moved into before there were any windows and doors. However the weather was warm and we seemed to get along.

4

Chapter 4

One day while Dad and Mother and the two oldest boys were away, a black bear came down to the creek that ran a few roads from the house on the north, Dora was the oldest, and of course we were scared. I was to small to climb the ladder to the upper floor, so Dora helped me up ahead of her and Jim and Amos followed, and they then drew the ladder up too, so the Bear could not climb up. We could watch her from the opening of the last upper window. She sat up on her haunches, and looked awhile, then ambled off back to the woods. Then the ladder was let down and we all came down, glad that she was not interested in trying to get us. About that time our parents were away one night until late, the two older boys were home, and were to go to a small meadow south about a quarter of a mile from the house to get hay for the oxen, and like boys, played and delayed until well after dark. Dora was afraid to stay at the house alone with me, so we went along with the boys who carried a lantern. While the boys got the hay together, and tied in bundles with ropes, Dora and I crouched under some low hanging brushes, keeping very still in our hiding place, we smelled a bear. The male bear have an odor not unlike that of a Billy Goat. When the boys were ready with the hay we were glad to get back with the lighted lantern. Also this same summer I think it was, that an animal came one dark night to the barn door, which was closed of course, and fastened on the outside. Father was away somewhere, but Mother was home, and the older boys too, and Herman and all of us went up stairs where we could get the best view of the barn. There was only two great gleaming eyes to be seen, about as high as a big bears head would be if it stood on it's hind feet, about 5 or 6 feet. But it could have been a cougar, as one was killed near by later. Herman took careful aim with a shot gun, and fired at the eyes, but of course shot scatters, and would not kill a bear that far away.

Father built his barn farther away than most men do. It was at least twice as far as my barn is from the house. Mother cooked out of doors that first winter, as the house was small, and we six children needed room to move around in. Mother had a big iron range, with six griddles, a plain space, and a reservoir. Dad built a shelter over the stove to keep the snow off, and of course the trees were so near the house, there was not much wind, we never had drifts like we do here. Mother managed to keep us in home knit wool stockings, and socks, but we never had long underwear, or extra warm clothes, and how Mother stood it to cook for eight people out of doors all winter I never can understand. The following summer Dad built a lean to kitchen on the west end of the house.

One night while we six children were making a lot of noise in the kitchen, and Dad and Mother were away, there was an awful scream over our heads in a huge Basswood that hung over the kitchen roof. (Silence in the kitchen) Then Herman grabbed the ever ready gun from the corner of the kitchen, stuck it out of the open window, aimed up towards the tree top and fired. We heard the animal hit the ground as it leaped from the tree, but daylight showed no blood, and the dry ground no tracks, so we never knew what it was but must have ben a Bob Cat, Lynx, or Cougar. They being the only large cats in that region.

It must have ben the following winter, because I was still a small girl, that Dad was sick in bed again, we were desperately in need of groceries again, which happened quite often. Father had made an ox yoke to order for a man near Rock Creek. The ox yokes Father made were beautiful in line and workmanship. I think they were carved from Birch logs, and were scraped smooth, then sandpapered, and rubbed to a high finish polish, at that time he had one about finished. He managed to get up and finish the polish, and the two older boys Herman and Tom, about

14 and 12 years old, loaded it onto a clumsy wooden homemade hand sled, and hauled it the 3 or 4 miles to the man who ordered it, hoping to get the money to buy flour and what else was needed. They left home fairly early of a winter day hauling the heavy yoke on a sled, but when they delivered it the man did not pay them for the yoke. He must have known the money was needed or the boys would not have hauled it so far by hand. It is possible the man did not have the money to pay with, as money was scarce at that time, and wages low, and pay slow in coming. When the boys returned they came with drooping heads, hating to tell Dad they didn't get the money, and I don't know if Dad ever got his pay for the ox yoke.

One day while I was still small, about five or six, Father came home from hunting. He wore a heavy coat, called a mackinaw at the time. He had something under his coat near his breast. He coaxed me to put my hand in there and feel it, Mother, fearful it was something that would bite me said "Now Honey" and Father said "It won't hurt her Mary". So reassured, I put my hand in and quickly withdrew it when I felt the smooth creature. I think I had expected to feel fur, but what Dad had brought home was a young crow. What that crow learned to do was marvelous. He learned to say "Ma" and "Pa", "Hello" and he picked out me as the one safest to tease, I being the smallest. When he could find me out doors alone he would flight on my head, pick me, and pull my hair. Then when I would cry, he would fly into the tall pines near the house and caw, and caw, making fun of me.

He would watch his chance and steal Mothers silver from the dining table when it was set for a meal. He would come hopping in the house thro the open door, sideways, just a hop at a time watching to see if anyone was near, and if not, he would fly up, pick up a spoon or fork, fly out, and hide it in the chips or grass. He would steal pieces of soap he could carry, and lead pencils. He could go to the stove pipe hole, in summer, poke his head in and say "Hello, hello, hello." He followed the boys when they went to hunt the cows in the woods, the cows wore a bell and it was free cattle range in the first few years, later Father and the boys built a rail fence.

He would watch his chance and steal mothers silver from the dining table when it was set for a meal, He would come hopping into the house thro the open door, sideways, just a hop at a time watching to see if any one was near, and if not he would fly up, pick up a spoon or fork, fly out, and hide it in the chips or grass. He would steal pieces of soap he could carry, and lead pencils, He would go to the stove pipe hole, in summer, poke his head in and say "Hello, hello, hello".

Somehow the crow loved to visit the Englishman in the early morning. It was a short flight for him, only one and a half miles, and he greeted them thro their stove pipe hole too. We heard the man had vowed to shoot him, yet he never did, as my Father became so enraged when Jack, (the crow), stole his last carpenter pencil, and flew into the pine tree. He (Dad) had snatched his gun from the wall, his aim was all too true and Jack gave his life for his thieving ways. We children cryed, and so did Mother and I imagine Dad was ashamed after he realized we all loved the naughty black fellow so much. Jim made a little wooden casket, and we had a burial of our own beloved pet, and Mother attended too. Later as vinegar grew low in the five gal. keg, where Mother kept her home made maple vinegar, and in the bottom was several of her cups she had missed and blamed we children for carrying them out, but what really happened was that she would reach into the hole in the top big enough for her hand and a cup, set the cup on the top and leave it there and the sly, jolly, Jack would poke it into the hole to hear it splash in the vinegar. I suppose he thought she could put a cup in the hole, he could too. We also found soap, spoons, and forks Jack had buried in the fine chips in the yard.

Along about this time an accident happened to my oldest Brother Herman, one day he was chopping some wood near the house about a hundred feet I would say, and his ax caught on the clothes line Mother had strung out there. The ax bounded back and struck him in the head, knocking him down and out for a short time. Happily Father and Mother were home, they carried him to the house, and dashed cold water in his face, and he came to, but if it had ben a double bitted ax as they sometimes used it would have ben curtains for him. While I was still very small there was a Civil War Vetrans Encampment at Pine City. Dad and Mother had a tent, and I being the baby of the family, Mother took me along, no doubt to make it easier for those at home. I remember the big bon fire of old barrelles and rubbish the boys made. They were "The Sons of Vetrans" an organization of the youths of the Civil War, sons of Soldiers. I can recall seeing Herman on a barrell rolling, and riding it like a Riverman rides a floating log. One evening Mother and I were visiting in the tent of a neighbor, and another woman named Russel and her little daughter. The same age as I was visiting there too, and Mr. Crawford brought a small sack of apples to treat his wife and children.

Mrs. Crawford handed the apples around to her children while Daisy Russel stood close in front of us silently waiting to see if she got one too. Daisy was an only child, and no doubt spoiled. When Mrs. Crawford had only one apple left, (her own), she gave it to Daisy, who turned to me triumphantly, and said "you can have half" I stood silently watching the scene, secretly ashamed of Daisy, even though she generously gave me half. Later Mother told me how proud she was of me because I had not acted like Daisy. Praise from my Mother was a rich reward for me always.

When I was about eight years old my Father was able to go to the lumbar woods to work as a handyman. Making Ox yokes, sleigh runners, Ox handles and whatever was needed in wood working. Mother and we three younger children were at home. The three older ones working out away from home. I don't recall what or where the older boys were. Dora was working for her board in Pine City and supposedly going to school but I doubt if she was sent to school steady as attendance was not compulsory at that time, and she worked for people who had babies and small children, and needed her help. No doubt Mother needed her at home too, but it would be one more mouth to feed. So she was at home very little after she was ten or twelve years old. Father being away, groceries and flour got low, and the flour gave out before thanksgiving. There was no bread for us at thanksgiving and very little else in the house. Neighbors were loyal in those days, even as they are now, so Mother sent Jim, (about fourteen at that time) to our neighbors named Franklin about three or four miles from us, to borrow flour. There was snow, and it was cold, but Jim took the empty sack and his gun and went to borrow flour, and boy like he lingered too long, and the night came early, and he was not home, and Mother began to worry, and of course we smaller children were scared too. I recall that Mother, Adolph, and I stood out in the chill air and looked and listened for his coming. Then to our straining ears and hearts came the long drawn bay of the Timber wolves, and we knew they had picked up Jims track and were following him. How long we waited and listened I don't know but it seemed hours at the time, while the wolf calls came nearer and nearer. Then came Jim into the clearing, carrying 25 pounds of flour on his back, and his gun. To me Jim has always ben a hero, because he did not drop the flour, and kept his head in time of danger. And what an ordeal for a mother, even for a short time. A few days later, Mr. Crawford came to see how we were getting along and Mother got a letter off to Dad. I think he came home soon after, and did not leave us again that winter.

5

Chapter 5

January 5th, 1959 I left this History of my life a year ago to write Historical stories for the State Granger. This story depends entirely on me as there is only my Brother Amos Austin, and I left of our family. Amos is 80 years old and has forgotten things that I can remember, but I will soon be 78 so I should hurry and finish this and get it up to date, because at least one of my Grandchildren wants it and she shall have it if I live to write it which I may not.

My Father was not an easy man to get along with, but Mother somehow managed to do so, even in poverty and real hardship. I remember waking up one morning while I was quite small, to find Mother sitting on my bed crying. I could hear Father storming around down stairs, and then he went out. I never knew what the fuss was about. Just one of his tempers I think. But to me my Mother seemed perfect, and what he could find to row about is beyond me. My Brother Jim was a Policeman in the City of Minneapolis for 35 years. He died at the old home of my Parents in Pine City of a Heart Attack. His second wife Ida lived there until she suffered a stroke and her son came and took her to New York. She too is passed away now, and her ashes rest near her two husbands in a cemetery in Minneapolis.

None of Jims children were at his funeral, as they couldn't stand their Stepmother, and no doubt never knew when he died. Unless a certain man I saw there dressed in a working mans clothes at the Cemetery could have ben his son Henry. I have often wished I had spoken to him as I had noticed how much he looked at me and that he greatly resembled my Brother Jim. If he was Henry Austin, he no doubt did not want to be recognized by his Stepmother.

Going back to my childhood, my interest in Birds and animals began when I was seven or eight years old. There was a Bluebirds nest in a hollow stump in our small field, and I was a daily visitor at the stump to peek down at the beautiful Bluebird who became so tame she would not fly from the nest, and I knew I must not touch the tiny baby birds. The pets I had were cats, and dogs and a Singer Canary. My Brothers would send the Dogs to chase my cats, to hear me yell. My Brother Tom never teased me but once, as far as I can remember, that time he hung my Dolly out the upstairs window with ink on its cheeks for tears, and I saw it when I came up the path from the pasture. Of course I cried, and he was sorry. He used to read my letters I wrote to my older Brother who was married when I was about ten. I would start a letter and leave it lying around until I was ready to finish it. Tom had fun reading them, until Mother put me wise, and I was more careful to conceal them. About this time my Brother Tom and Dad had a quarrel over something and Tom left home. I never knew what it was all about, but Mother cried all night, and was so heart broken that Dad scoured the neighborhood, a matter of ten or twelve miles to locate him. He learned he was with a friend of the family named Van Gordon. Then Mother was satisfied, as we all was fond of Mr. Van Gordon. He came quite often to visit our house, I guess he was lonely too as he was a Batcheler. He was married in middle life, and I think later took his family to some Eastern State where he came from before we knew him. I think he felt sorry for we children because he brought us candy, and if he met Dad in town he would send candy to us.

Sometime after my Husband and I moved to the southern part of the State I went back home to visit my parents and niece who lived with them. My niece and I went to a movie. We saw Mr. Van Gordon there and I went and spoke to him as I knew he would not recognize me. When I told him who I was, he stared at me and said “You look old”.

It was like a slap in the face, as I was still girlish looking and used to being admired and treated with respect. Did the old Goat think I was running after him? He was old enough to be my father. It was simply that he had ben kind to we children, and I thought he would be glad to see me.

To return again to my childhood- there were swamps twenty miles long in Pine County and one bay about one half mile south of Fathers farm. Moss hung in long streamers from the tall Tamarack trees, and the moss under foot was soft and damp, yellow moccasin flowers grew there, and the boys often brought some home when they came from hunting, then came the forest fires and burned out the swamps killing the Tamarack trees, and leaving the swamps dead with many down trees and what fires they were, flames to the top of the tallest trees and leaping fifteen to twenty feet in the air. When the first fire came, the smoke was so dense that Mother and the writer went into the cellar to get out of the smothering atmosphere. The mid day seemed like twilight, and yet Father and Amos fought fire alone, the three other boys were away. Dad set back fires and watched to put out any sparks that would be carried across by the force of the heat. I don't remember that there was any wind. It was hot and dry and the pitch in the trees made the fire much more fierce than hard wood timber would make. Amos was just a boy at that time twelve or thirteen years old, but he fought manfully beside Dad until the fires had roared past, and the home was safe. Then Mother put cold packs on their eyes to soothe them and draw out the inflammation, and what a relief when it was over and the dense smoke cleared some, so one could breathe more easily. The pond in the swamp dried up after the trees died, and all the beautiful tiny fish were no more. We never knew where the fountain head of this small pond was or how the fish got there in the beginning. It must have ben the dim dark ages after the last Ice Age. I have never seen any fish like them, all so tiny. Brown and copper colored. One spring the creek rose to the width of a small River. The creek was near our house on the lower ground. The older boys went fishing in the Boat. Amos and I were playing along the edge of the water where it flooded up on the grass, and two fine Pickerel came swimming along side by side, having some difficulty in the shallow water and grass. Amos grabbed a pole lying near that was used sometimes to push the Boat, and he struck the fish on the back stunning them, then jumped in and threw them out on the dry land. The big boys came home without any fish, and Amos was so proud of his two nice fish.

Our house was small, probably about 15 by 20 feet and one story and a half. I loved to listen to the rain on the roof in the summer. The winter I was twelve years old my folks kept Boarders, so I slept down stairs on a pallet on the floor. I had to arise at 5: at morning, and help Mother get breakfast, then there was all those dishes to wash, but I grew fat, was a real tubby. I suppose I ate too much cake and pie, as Mother set out good meals.

My sister Dora was married when I was about ten years old. She had worked in the City of Minneapolis the winter before, but did not like the city, so came home in the spring, and a Batcheler spied her, and he came and courted her, and they were married in the fall. They lived with us that winter and her husband (Monroe Shuey) built a house in the spring half way from our house to Pine City. I remember that wedding as tho it was a short time ago. She was married at home by a justice of the Peace, named Stone. At that time he had a hotel in Pine City. Before my sister went to the City to work. She had ben a waitress or as they were then called “a Dining Room Girl”. She was very pretty slender, brown eyed, with rich brown hair, and fair skin. The type of girl hotel keepers liked for waitresses. I don’t think she worked there very long. She was too shy for such a place, and she did not like the men who came there to eat. The country was new, and many of the men were loggers, and drifters and rough and rough spoken. After she was married and had a big house and two Babies, I stayed with her awhile, and took care of the Babies morning and night while she milked cows. Her husband did not like to milk, anyway they only had one cow at that time. Dora made butter to sell in town, price was ten cents per lb. Eggs seven cents a dozen, and calico was five cents a yard, Gingham was 10 cents.

This was during the Cleveland Administration. Dora would carry her butter to Pine City on foot, as the team of colts were not broke to drive at that time. That same year my Brother Tom was married to a Girl named Mary Jackson, a Norwegian. They got along fine until her parents moved from Wisconsin and bought some land adjoining Fathers Farm. Tom had met her some years before when her family lived in Pine City before they moved to Wisconsin. Then Tom went over to Wisconsin to see her, and on his return the Ferry was not running so he swam the St. Croix River. He must have picked up a germ because he came down with Typhoid Fever. Somehow I got on her nerves not intentionally, for I adored Tom, but I probably was too talkative, so I was sent to my sister Dora's, and stayed there until Tom was able to sit up.

The Girl Tom married, and I got along fine as long as they lived together, but Mary's parents moved over to Minnesota, and soon after that the trouble began. Times were hard, and very little work to be had to bring in money, and Mary became unhappy, and discontented and kept leaving Tom and going to her folks. She had a sweet Baby Girl with big brown eyes, and dark curly hair. When Baby was about 18 months old she left him the third time, and he wouldn't ask her to come back again, as he had before. He left Pine County and came to Dodge Co. as we had friends here who had lived in Pine County near us.

When Clara (The Baby) became very sick and she (Mary) and her folks thought she was about to die. She wanted Tom to take the Baby, Tom was in Dodge County at that time. So Father and Mother drove out there and brought the child home with them. She had "Cholera Infantum" as it was called then, also was "anemic" as her pretty brown hair was faded to a straw color. They stopped at my sister Dora's on their way home, and the writer was shocked at the sight of the boney little body. I was staying at my sister Dora's for a week or so, and saw her the day they brought her home.

When Clara (The Baby) became very sick and she, Mary and her folks thought she was about to die. She wanted Tom to take the Baby, Tom was in Dodge County at that time, So Father and mother drove out there and brought the child home with them, She had "Cholera Infantum" as it was called then; also was anemic"

Later after my parents had cared for her and she was well and plump, her mother wanted her back, but my parents would not give her up, then followed a law suit, but the Doctor who had treated her, told in court of her condition at the time my parents took her, and the judge gave her to her Grandparents. A neighbor woman testified of how she knew the Baby had lain in filth in the night, not being changed or cared for. This Girl lived with her Grandparents until her Grandmother died, then she came to live with the writer until she was married. She did not live to see her three children grow up, but died at thirty two. She requested to be buried in our local cemetery near our house, and she knew the "Auntie" she so dearly loved would visit her grave and mourn her early passing.

I must now return to my early childhood and the deep snows of winter, and the joys of summer when we camped and picked wild Black berries, and Blueberries, and caught fish in the Snake River, and the St. Croix River. How I loved the call of the whippoorwill, in the cool of the evening, and I cuddled close to Mother when the Timberwolves across the River in Wisconsin would send out their long drawn bay or call. We camped at what was called the dead water, on the Snake River, the water was still and deep there, and Blackberries grew rampant there, also wild Blueberries. But after the big fires burned it off, it killed out the wild fruit, also burned up the huge Pine down logs that had fallen in a time long past, but preserved from decay by the great amount of Pitch they contained. It must have made a terrible hot fire, some of these logs were three feet at the base. There was no standing timber for a half mile back from the River, and several miles along its shores as I remember it. But it has ben sixty five years since I was there, so I cannot be for sure of distances.

EPILOGUE

Olive Birdie Austin Smith belonged to the Wasioja Baptist Church and was an active member of her community. Wasioja was a farming community, and the people that lived in the area were always helping each other out. It was very common to help your neighbors with their children, or to make a meal for them, or to help with farm work, or to help take care of them when they or a family member were sick. I believe this is where the saying "it takes a village" comes from, because everyone in the village helped each other out.

Birdie married her husband, Clarence Elmar Smith (Clair), on June 28th, 1894, in Wisconsin. Their first son Elton Lavern Smith (my great grandfather), was born in Pine City, MN on June 11th, 1895. Soon after, they settled on a farm in Wasioja, Minnesota, where they farmed and raised their family. Their second son, Monroe Franklin Smith, was born April 8th, 1900, and their adopted daughter, Majorie Ruth Smith, was born November 25th, 1916. They also had two sons that I believe were either still born or passed away shortly after birth.

Birdie's niece Clara lived with them after Birdie's mother, Mary, passed away in 1913. She lived with them until she married in 1915.

Their youngest son, Monroe, was born with a condition called methemoglobinemia (Blue Baby Syndrome). This condition causes their skin to look blue due to the lack of oxygen in their blood. They were told that he wouldn't live past the age of one. He defied all odds and lived to the age of eighteen. He passed away on January 11th, 1919, at the age of 18.

Elton married Nellie Hindal in 1925, and they made their home on the family farm where they farmed with his parents and raised their seven children: Valera, Clarence, Lawrence, Stanley, Roberta (my grandma), Ellwynn, and Barb. Elton passed away on February 17th, 1960 at the age of 64.

Marjorie married Merton Bartel in 1933 and settled on a farm in Byron, MN. They had nine children: Merton, Evelyn, Sharon, Donald, Shirley, Forest, Clarence, Lawrence, and Daniel. Margie passed away on November 20th, 2002.

Birdie's husband, Clair, passed away December 17th, 1947, at the age of 76. Birdie passed away at her home on December 5th, 1966.

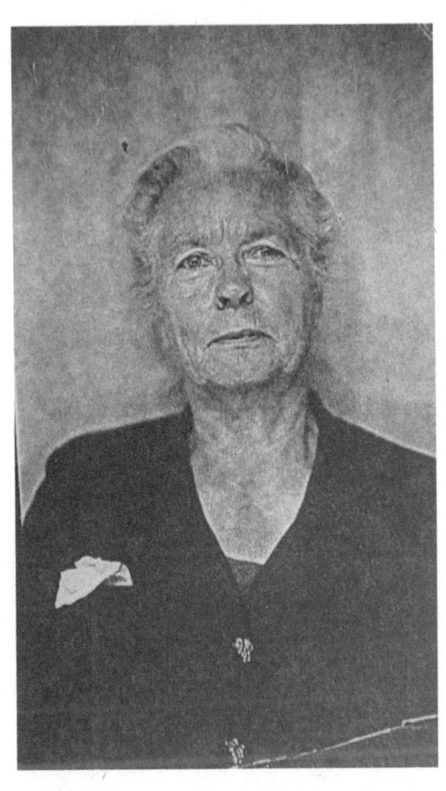

DAY DREAMS

On a mossy bank by a singing river
Where trees drop over and kiss the stream
Let me rest there from earths deep sorrow
Let me hide for a day to dream

Let me forget there are those who love me
Let me forget there is pain to bear-
Let me rest my eyes on the skies above me
Let me rest my heart in prayer

Then when at last my heart is rested
Then when at last my tears are dried-
I will turn once more to work neglected
I will use the strength which God provides

LOVE

I love the gentle breezes
That lift the flower faces and the leaves
Upon the trees
The smooth and soft fragrance that comes
Upon the air
And the scent of lovely flowers
Wafted everywhere
I love the rolling thunder, that bursts upon the night
Arousing me from slumber, in sudden wild fright
The rain drops loudly beating upon the roof and window pane
I love the pouring rain-
I love the happy Robbins that fleet among the trees
The tiny house wren singing up high in the leaves
The saucy blue jay calling from off the garden wall
I love them all

ROBINS FAREWELL

This morning as I staked the goat
To fill itself on mast
I heard a robin in a tree
Calling summer's past
It seemed to me a mournful sound
To hear at dawn of day
A robin calling to his mate
"Come on, let's fly away"

The summer's spent, the air grows chill
The sun is more remote
No more we'll hear a song of cheer
From robin's russet throat

A sad good-bye, away they fly
To warmer, sunnier lands
I'm left behind, a goat to mind
And warm my chilling hands

MEMORIES OF CHILDHOOD

I see an old stone wall with willows bending o'er
A cozy little cottage with ivy round the door
A chuckling little brook that wanders through the hills

The shades of falling night and the call of whippoorwills
I dream a wooded hill against the evening sky-
A meadow lush and sweet, with cattle standing by
A wild doe at the brook, to gaze and drink her fill

Again I dream of the call of the whippoorwill
I dream I see the boys come trooping in at eve
Turn in their collared shirts, roll up their worn out sleeves
And then splash and shine of water sprinkled o'er
The back steps and the bench beside the kitchen door
They laugh and joke and scuffle comes back to me again

Though many years have passed, since these boys grew to men
These memories round me throng
And haunt the closing day - Though many years have passed
And these boys are old and gray

ALONE

There's a plot on a hill just one mile away
Keeps calling to me, by night and by day
The four I have loved lie silently there
While I dwell alone, in grief and despair

My loss has not lessened through the long lonely years
I sit here alone with my prayers and tears
My hope for the future has vanished from life
I sit here alone - once a mother and a wife

TO MY LOST HUSBAND

I dreamed you held me to your heart
Beside the ocean wide
And while you held me to your breast
I bowed my head and cried

Because I'd missed you oh so much
While you were far away
And while you held me in your arms
I thought you had come to stay

And then I wakened from my dreams
And found that you had died
And now my tears are not a dream
I bowed my head and cried

TO MY SON MONROE

You are gone from my life
And a shadow fills my heart
The brightness is gone from the noon-time
The midnight seems more dark

I arose from fillful dreaming
And from my slumber starts
I heard you calling "Mother"
Fancy of a hungry heart

Out in the cold bleak winter night
I stand with arms out - stretched
To that distant hill where you lie alone
And no one knows my sorrow or hears my moan

Out of the memories of the past
Comes your dear head on my breast
Your arms about my neck
after hours of unrest

Lest to me on earth
But in the still dark hours of the night
Apart from the stress of day
Comes the notes of "Star of the East"
From your fingertips
Over my heart to stray

Soon I shall join you
In that peaceful rest
Would that I might pillow your head
Upon my breast

DEATH AT LAST

Nothing on earth is lasting
Nothing is here to stay
Everything earthly must parish
Must silently slip away

The snow in the distant mountain
The quivering aspen leaves
The dragon-fly skimming in the fountain
The song-star in the trees

The beautiful rose in the garden
Whose petals dropped one by one
The maid who walks with her lover
And has her place in the son

But kindly words may linger
And pass from heart to heart
Unselfish acts may flourish
That from humble natures start
Great love may last forever
When a king from his throne steps down
For love of a lovely woman
Who may not share his crown
Thus love is stronger than kingdoms

And love is deeper than night
For it comes from our heavenly Father
And follows us in our flight

TO MY DEAR HUSBAND

It is eight long years since you were here
To cheer me with your presence, dear
Yet, though you sleep on snow clad hill
Your spirit lingers with me still

And now that I have passed the year
That you had not when you were here
My love is just as great and true
As it was the day I married you

I sit alone and wonder when
The time will come when we will meet again
My love will be as strong and true
As the day I said "I do"

IN MEMORY OF CLAIR

I sit alone in the evening
As the day draws to its close
Darkness falls o'er the garden
As the dew falls on the rose

And in my heart is shadows
Like the darkness on the lawn
As I dream of you my darling
In the light of the days beyond
And in my heart is the memory
Of your last week, sweet caress
As I wiped death's dew from your forehead
And prayed above your breast

You are gone but not forgotten
I am yours forever more
Till night cease to fall o'er the garden
And waves cease to lap the shores

APRIL

There's a robins nest in the old oak tree
And a bluebird flashes by
The woodpecker drums a loud ta-too
Then voices his raven's cry

A gentle rain (tis nature's tears)
Drips down from the skies of God
It waters the earth and the new green grass
Springs from the bare brown sod

The sun sinks low in the glowing west
The sparrows softly chirp
Then night comes down with silent wings
And folds all softly to sleep

FRESHMAN (TO VALERA)

Ready for high school, this maiden fair
With the gray-blue eyes, and nut-brown hair
Young and carefree, dear and sweet
From curly hair to rosy feet
Into the future the gray eyes gaze
Life is leading to unknown ways
Darling, I love you! God keep your days
From all the dangers that beset your ways

LINES TO MY DEAR CLARA

I wonder in the shadow of the dark and solemn pines
Tonight my heart is sad and lone
Raindrops murmur "Clara", she is many miles away

But I know her loving heart is here at home
O, Come to me, dear Clara, in the silent hours of the night,

While visions fair beguile my weary brain
Come whisper words of comfort to my sad and lonely heart
Sweet murmurs like the patter of the rain

TO MY COUSIN LEONA CROSS

Though space may divide us
For many a mile, I'll still love you truly

Please grant me your smile
In sending you this daisy

I'm wishing your right well
My only sweet cousin
My sweet Leona Belle

THE OLD HIGH CHAIR

This old highchair, to me so dear
Has stood the test of time and of tears

To me it could not be more dear
If it should last a thousand years

The seven children it has held
Now all grown up and gone their ways

But still to me this chair remains
Remembrance of other days

I'll wash it off and polish it up
It's arms and legs and seat and all
The while I breathe a secret prayer
For my grandchildren grown so tall

WANDERLUST

Be happy where you are, O heart of mine
The freshness of the dewy morn
The stars that shine from out the midnight sky
All, all are mine

Think not of distant lands
Dream not of ships at sea
Think only of those near and dear
And be content with me

The time and place forbid you wander far
Fix your hungry gaze upon the evening star
And know that God has willed you here to stay
Not let your longing steal you far away

TO MY SON ELTON
(A BABY ONE YEAR OLD)

A gleam of sunshine, a lot of joy
A frolicsome dimpled baby boy
A fleeting glimpse of fairy's wings
Happiness such as cherubs bring
A golden note of an angels song
Joy and smiling the whole day long

Eyes of blue and sunny hair
Cupid mouth in sweetness rare
Rounded limbs so soft and so neat
Marvel of plumpness his body sweet
This is our darling, all complete

OUT OF THE PAST

Out of the deep dark shadows of an untold past
Comes the neanderthal man
Emerged at last from torrid heat into a cooler land
Which fosters the growth and soul of man

And not alone, for by his side
Staunch and fearless came - his captive bride
Fair in the morning light of that far day
She saw the rising sun then knelt to pray

No other God she knew, but in her heart
She thought the sun must live in part
She wore no robe or cloth attire
She seemed to move in living fire

Her long golden hair in rippling sheet
Concealed her form so round and sweet
Her dimpled knees and bare brown feet
Seemed shyly playing "Hide and seek"

Her lord was built so tall and square
With flowing build and raven hair
His brooding eyes so dark and grave
Be spoke a soul so proud and brave
Her azure eyes now open wide
To find him kneeling by her side

He shudders now sick and afraid
Seeing the bruise his bludgeon made
There close beside her bosom fair
And half concealed by golden hair

The day wore on as all days do
Her fears beset her anguish grew
And nature seemed to meet her mood
Losing her furies on the wood
He saw his fair and gentle wife
Grow clumsy with a coming life
And sabers coat so bright and warm
Was often repaired to fit her form
And often returning from his snares

Her lord brought pelts of squirrel and hares
And these she shyly hid away
Made ready for a future day

The friendly creatures of the air
Built nests about the hidden lair
The squirrels and monkeys in the trees
Came so boldly forth to scold and tease

The monkeys and the squirrels were tame
The man went far to trap his game
She seeks her lair with hasty tread
And sitting down upon her bed
A bed of grass pulled from the slough
She ponders her fears anew

Then quickly from some pelts thrown down
She picks one out to build a gown
A shapeless thing of sudden need
Bound to her form with lengths of reed
She seeks the lake-let cave once more

And kneeling there upon the shore
She sees the pelt of saber tooth
Enhance her charms in very truth

Now satisfied she hastens back
To seek her mate in forest track
As any modern maid would do
Sends out a joyous loud hello

Her lord returning from his snare
Is weighted down with family cares
The game is scarce, the snares unsprung
Though cunningly concealed and hung

A sudden stirring in the wood
He rouses from his pensive mood
The lovely woman cooked his meat
And kept her cave clean and neat
But time sped on, as all time will
At night the cave grew cold, then chill

Her time had come, her fears grew wild
She knew she was to bear a child
The night was dark, the cave grew chill
And torrents fell o'er wood and hill
A giant tree from great roots tore
Was thrown across the cavern door

Her kingly lord, unknown to pain
Pays little head to the wind and rain
Wrapped his pelt of mountain sheep
Lays calmly down and goes to sleep

The little wife conceals her fears
And tries to drown her pain in tears
Moves softly from her husband's side
Thus her pain and tears to hide

The rising sun, the woods to lave
Shines far into the dismal cave
And in the corner rough and wild
Reveals the mother with her child

Clasped close within her warm embrace
His hunting club hung by his side
Secured by belt and string of hide
The ugly hammer chipped from stone
Swung from a handle made of bone

Thus standing in the morning light
They made a fair and cheerful sight
The brawny man with raven hair
The winsome lass with tresses hair

And scampering around the maid and man
Was a small monkey furred in tan
Loving to tease the noble pair
He pulled the womans golden hair
Nipped the mans toes and running up
Perched upon his raven top

The man departs to tend his snares
And leaves her to the home cave cares
So close within the watery cave
She seeks her fair young form to lave

Up from the lake-let shining clear
Her face and bosom both appear
And starting back in sudden shame
A fear is born, she cannot name

Grasping his club with closer grip
Slyly through the brush he slips
He sees a tawny shade he knows
Its saber tooth his worst of foes
He throws his club with brawn and skill
And hopes to make a bloody kill

An anguish cry, a strangled moan
This lord of earth seems turned to stone
He quickly hears his victims side
And finds it is his golden bride

He picks her up in arms like steel
And swiftly through the jungle reels
He bears lightly as he runs

As though she were a doe or fawn
He takes her to the lake-let shore
And in deep anguish brooding o'er
He gently lave the face so fair
And presses back the golden hair

What is it then that makes him start
And draw his bearded lips apart
The pelt of saber tooth he sees
From bosom swell to dimpled knees

He stares to see his golden bride

All wrapped with tigers hide
He sees a tiny baby face
That closely to the mother pressed
Draws liquid from her breast

The son grows tall, and strong and brave
With knowledge of the woods and caves
And fleet of foot and sharp of eye
And quick to hear old sabers cry

And prouder than his mom or sire
He knows desserts his home care fire
And wandering far from parents cave
Becomes a warrior strong and brave

THE MAID OF OLD STONE AGE

We read of the man of the old stone age
His courage and his skill
We see him creep through forests deep
To make his bloody kill

We see him fight with all his might
To win his right to live
We see him sleep in caverns deep
With naught but love besides

But who of the "Maid of the old stone age"
Who wandered by his side
Who had her share of grief and care

THE CAMP OF SNAKE RIVER

Softly now the shades of evening
Deepen into night
Hear the whippoorwills sad calling
Through the starry night

All the trees across the river
Drown in the silver hills
Soft the doe steps to the water
Drinks her dainty fill

Far away the long drawn baying
Call the wolf king's pack
Hungry forms among the bushes
Steal along her track

Then the doe, her soft eyes startled
Hears the wolf king's call
Swims among the foamy current
Thus escapes them all

BIRD CRADLE

An orioles nest in the maple trees
Securely hidden away from me
I dream of it by night, I search for it by day
In the tall old maple across the way

I know it's there - High on the tree
Cleverly hidden among the leaves
Cradling eggs or nestling fair
Kissed by the sunshine, rocked by the breeze

Soon the bird-lings will all be grown
Plump and feathered each will be
Loving the cradle high in the sunshine
Flitting lightly through the trees

TO THE OCEAN

O, Ocean I have loved you from afar
Distant, remote. As I have loved the evening star
And then I beheld you - Love became pain
A love intense and dear, like the distant star
But close and sweet

Your green waves, breaking at my feet
O, Ocean you have won me, I am ever thine
Though far away, I worship your shrine

THE DEAD MILL

Alone, moss-grown, abandoned
It stands in the woods by the stream
The old mill that was once so busy with grain
Hauled a long distance by team

The wheel now hangs useless and silent
It's paddles are broken to shreds
The flooring is rotten and crumbled to dust
The old mill stands lonely and dead

Its glory has vanished forever
Its doors on their hinges sag low
While out from its sad broken windows
The chipmunks and squirrels come and go

The bats fly about it at twilight
And sleep in its shadows by day
And I sigh for the mill its in hay-day
And the ruins are left to decay

THE COUNTRY DOCTOR

Out of the cold dark night
Out of the storm and stress
Comes a call for help-
The Doctor's "S.O.S."
Out of his nice warm bed-
Into his clothes he leaps
Gathering coat and grip
While he's half asleep

His wife comes to the door
A pleading look in her eyes
"Must you go out in the storm?"
"Yes, I must go," he replies

"A child needs my care
A mother is in distress
Dear one, go back to bed
You must have your rest"

He hurries his horses out
He hitches them to the sleigh
Now he is on his way
The storm is getting worse
The blizzard is getting wild
But he must hurry along
To attend to a woman and child

The team has lost the road
They are wallowing in a drift
The doctor climbs out in the snow
To give his team a lift

Alone in the dark and storm
He shovels best he can
He finally gets them out
He's now a superman
Arrived at the place of call
He blankets his team with care
He knows that they are tired and cold
He hates to leave them there

The night wears on apace
The dawn begins to gleam
The doctor needs food and rest
But thinks of his waiting team

No shelter is provided them here
No measure of grain or hay
He wearily dons his coat
And starts his homeward way

The snow is now knee deep
The road unbroken lies
The doctor turns his team
And sadly, deeply sighs

OLD MA GOOSE

I feel so guilty each time I meet
The old Ma Goose with waddling feet
On Sunday morn (it was no use)
But I backed the car over old Pa Goose
I was too fast, as most folks are
When I pressed the gas in the big red car

And old Pa Goose, as I backed around
Defied the car on my own night ground
When I returned in an hour or less
I found him breathing his last short breath

"Twas Sunday morn, but all that day
I plucked Pa Goose in a tearful way
A broken wing was not worth saving
It went to the cat to ease her craving
But when at eve I had him dressed
With sorry heart, I went to rest
The old Ma Goose gives me no blame

She tags me around and calls his name
In goose tongue I hear her say
"Come back, come back, my dear, I pray."

At night I hear her call her mate
It wakens me, both early and late
But poor Pa Goose has gone to stay
In a deep dark freeze he rests today
And now dear friends, keep this in mind
When you back your car, please look behind

LIGHTS AFAR

I like the people in our town
I like their shiny lights
They help cheer me when I'm blue
On dark and stormy nights

I sit up on this hill top
The village lies afar
And yet their lights shine out for me
Like friendly open doors

So leave your curtains up, dears
Your lights all shining bright
To comfort ole and lonely hearts
On a dark or stormy night

THE RUIN

I stood beside the ruin
As evening shadow fell
I seemed to hear the echo
Of the ancient rusty bell
I saw a ghostly company
File through the door
And then I heard such music
As I never heard before

The sweetest heavenly music
That flooded o'er my soul
As floods the sandy beaches
Beneath the ocean roll
I turned to gaze in wonder
At the woodland, straight and wild
And then I saw the graveyard
Beside the tumbling pile
All overgrown with ivy
And wild clematis sweet

I saw the crumbling monuments
Beside the great oakes feet
I saw the weeping willow
Bent o'er a humble stone
I stooped to read the name theron
"Sweet blue eyed Sally Austin
Is sleeping beneath this tree
She broke her heart for William
He who was lost at sea".

As I knelt in pity
Beside this grassy mound

I saw a tiny grave-let
Quite near it on the ground
"Rebecca Sally Austin",

The name seemed thus to be
"The child of blue-eyed Sally
And William lost at sea"

Now deep in meditation
I heard a sobbing sigh
I turned and there beside me
A man standing by
A dark and handsome stranger
Stood gazing at the mound
I said "Who are you mister
And why this sobbing sound?"

He said "Sweet Sally Austin
Was once my bonnie bride
And this our little daughter
Is sleeping by her side"

"This blue-eyed Sally Austin
She broke her heart for me
For, I, kind ma'am, am William
The William lost at sea"
When these few words were spoken
He vanished from my sight
And left me there by Sally's grave
In the departing light
As I stood there entranced, sir
A vision seemed to rise
Of gentle Sally Austin

With tearful deep blue eyes

Against her soft white bosom
She clasped a sleeping child
She stood and gazed upon me
"My dear kind friend", she murmured
"Why desecrate this sod?
This resting place is sacred
To sleepers and God"

I turned and stumble hastened
To my car beneath a tree
And left that spot, to shades of Sally
And of William "Lost at sea"

GYPSY BLOOD

There is a part of me that is tramp
A gypsy if you will
A part that longs to wander
Over distant vale and hill
I gaze on far horizons
And let my fancy roam
And then there is another part
That wants to stay at home

I hear the wild goose honking
Away up in the sky
It is then I wish that nature
Had willed me wings to fly
To visit distant mountains
And by wild torrents stray
There's surely no denying
I long to fly away
And then this other mother
That in my nature dwells

Looks happy about me
And tells me "all is well"
There is nothing to discourage me
Or cause my heart to roam
I am feeling quite content
It is best to be at home
I'll stay and tend the baby
While the family goes to town
I'll wash the stack of dishes
And bake the bread so brown
I'll feed the baby chickens
And see my days slip by

The while my heart is flying
Away up in the sky

NIGHT OF THE MINNESOTA BLIZZARD

This is a night for thinking
This is a night to pray
For those who are out and far from home
Upon the dark highways
God pity the sick and homeless
And young who have wandered far
From a light set in the window
Like a shining beckoning star

God comfort those who are worried
God answer those who pray
For loved ones caught in a snow drift
Out on the cold highway

Thank God for the true hearts yearning
Thank God for the true hearts praying
For those who are lost on the highways of life
There is always our God who care

FISHY TAILS

Come on, let's go fishing
Down by babbling brook
I'll bring some wiggly worms for bait
You fetch a line and hook
I'll pack some buns and cookies
You'll make some lemonade
We'll picnic there upon the bank
In the big old willow's shade
Maybe we'll catch a shiner
Perhaps a bullhead, too
Cleaned and fried for supper
They'll do for me and you
We'll sit beside the fire
And tell some fishy tales
And when at last, we both roll in
We'll dream we are catching whales

THE THIEF

I saw a naughty red squirrel
Running up a tree
He peeked into a knot hole
As saucy as could be

He said I'm very hungry
Some bird's eggs would taste fine
But too late, he saw his mistake
And tried to climb down

Pa Red - Head was too quick for him
And round and round he flew
And pecked him here, pecked him there
And whipped him black and blue
Soon joined by Mother Red - Head
She too, took up the flight
And picked that squirrely hard and fast
'Till down he fled in fright
Then joined by Madam Blue Jay

They pledged their friendship free
And one and all took up the flight
And chased him down the tree
He scampered here
And darted there

Not knowing what to do
For all around on every side
The angry allies flew

At last he spied a wood pile
And running hard and fast

He reached that haven, safe but sore
A wiser squirrel at last

He learned to dine on birds eggs
Is a rather costly fair
As Pa and Ma Red-Head
Had none they wished to spare

REMEMBRANCES

I remember the summer when I was a child
And my home near Pine City in the woods that were wild

The clearing my father had made on the land
In beautiful woods that to me were so grand

I remember when the birds nest I visited each day
In an old hollow stump, the nest made of hay
The tiny wee eggs and bird-lings I loved
I saw them each day as I gazed from above
The mother bird that trusted me, of that I am sure
She sat calmly on her nest as I gazed in her door
But the bird-lings grew strong, all feathered and plump
And left me the empty nest in the stump

OH HEART OF MINE

If your heart is hungry day by day
For scenes of earth that are far away
If you may not travel the wide world o'er
You can find rich treasures near your door

The moss that grows on the stones by the brook
The violets that nod in the shady brook
The nest that swings from the elm tall
The thrill of the whippoorwills evening call

Build your happiness wherever you are
The scented breeze, the evening star
The smile of a friend, a child's caress
These are the things that heal and bless

DROWNED CHILDREN

Across the ocean waves
We hear a pleading cry
America gives us homes
Hasten, are we die

Could outstretched arms of love
Their heavenward flight detain?
No! Englands children take their place
Among the neartered slain
Singing and stout of heart
They brave the stormy deep

Down to watery graves
Where unsung heroes sleep
Dear Mr. Roosevelt, who art our president,
Hallowed by thy name, Thy kingdom come
They will be done in the United States as things are done in Russia
Give us this day our daily bread and forgive
Us our bank robbing, kidnapping, and boozing
As we forgive ourselves
Lead us not into prosperity, but deliver us
From labor, for thine is the power, the hour
And the glory thereof forever

AUTUMN LEAVES

One by one the leaves come dancing
As the autumn leaves advancing
Catch them from the home tree straying
Shyly from the boughs a playing

All their colors brightly showing
Through the air come drifting, blowing
Forcing on our hearts the knowing
That autumn days are here

All the birds have ceased their singing
To far lands have wandered winging
We no longer see them springing
From every wayside tree

Soon old winter will come tramping
To my very door come stamping
With his cold and icy fingers
Lay his clutching hands on mine

LET YOUR LIGHT SHINE

Let me live in a house by the side of the road
And keep my windows bright
For those who pass along the way
On a dark and gloomy night

There are those who live in cloistered walls
With curtains closely drawn
Forgetting those who pass that way
Between the eve and dawn

Let me live in my house with windows bared
For those who pass my way
For the weary and worn, for the sad and forlorn
Who pass at the close of day

With windows bright and shining light
That throws its beams afar
May my light shine out to the weary world
Like the gleam of the evening start

www.ingramcontent.com/pod-product-compliance
Ingram Content Group UK Ltd.
Pitfield, Milton Keynes, MK11 3LW, UK
UKHW012248290726
14090UKWH00013B/536

9 798330 494392